THE
CURSE OF EARLY SUCCESS

REBALANCE, REPAIR, AND RESTORE THE SUCCESS YOU ONCE ENJOYED

ERIC JESSEN

Copyright © 2026 by Eric Jessen
First Paperback and Hardback Edition

All rights reserved. No part of this publication may be reproduced, distributed, or transmitted in any form or by any means, including photocopying, recording, or other electronic or mechanical methods, without the prior written permission of the publisher, except in the case of brief quotations embodied in critical reviews and certain other noncommercial uses permitted by copyright law. For permission requests, write to the publisher, addressed "Attention: Permissions Coordinator," at the address below.

Some names, businesses, places, events, locales, incidents, and identifying details inside this book have been changed to protect the privacy of individuals.

Published by Freiling Agency, LLC.

P.O. Box 1264
Warrenton, VA 20188

www.FreilingAgency.com

PB ISBN: 978-1-969826-30-6
HB ISBN: 978-1-969826-31-3
E-book ISBN: 978-1-969826-32-0

Contents

Introduction		v
Prologue	A Necessary Confession	xi
Chapter 1	The Curse of Early Success	1
Chapter 2	The Agentic-Communal Dial: Leading with Strength and Balance	9
Chapter 3	Complacency and the Dangers of Completion	19
Chapter 4	The Social Backlash of Success	25
Chapter 5	Slowing Down without Losing Speed	31
Chapter 6	Turning Rivals into Allies	41
Chapter 7	The Invisible Skills of Sustained Success	49
Chapter 8	Tools for Transformation	59
Chapter 9	Embracing Setbacks As Fuel	69
Chapter 10	Rediscovering Hands-On Learning	77
Chapter 11	Practicing Patience and Inclusivity in Collaboration	85
Chapter 12	Developing Emotional Intelligence and Self-Awareness	95
Chapter 13	Building Allies, Not Enemies	105
Chapter 14	Balance	113
Epilogue	From Shadow to Light	119

Early success,
If left unchecked,
can plant
the very seeds
of later downfall.

Introduction

We live in a world that celebrates the prodigy. From childhood, we are told that being ahead of the curve is the surest sign of future greatness. Schools praise it, companies reward it, and society writes stories about it. But what if the very thing that makes us exceptional early on is the same thing that sabotages us later? Early success, if left unchecked, can plant the very seeds of later downfall.

This book was born of that question and my own hard lessons. It is not written from the perspective of an expert with polished answers, but from someone who struggled to make sense of why the very qualities that once propelled me forward later seemed to hold me back.

Still, I've learned that those same seeds, when tended with awareness, can grow into humility and wisdom. What once felt like loss has often become preparation for something more profound. Along the way, I've been shaped not only by my own failures but by the grace of others—mentors who believed in me, family who steadied me, friends and colleagues who reminded me that growth is a team effort, not a solo race.

Still, I want to say something up front, as honestly as I can: this book is not for everyone. There are people, perhaps you are one of them, who have been gifted from birth with empathy, patience, kindness, and the ability to build harmony wherever they go. For such people, much of what follows may feel obvious, even simplistic. You may read certain pages and wonder why something so self-evident even needed to be written down. If that is the case, I envy you and admire you. Please do not take your strengths for granted. They are rare gifts, and **the world is better because of them.**

If you find yourself in that category, this book may offer something of value, though in a different way. It may help you understand peers, friends, or family members who do not carry those natural strengths, who instead wrestle with impatience, intensity, or a need to prove themselves. For them, what comes easily to you can be an exhausting, lifelong climb. This book can give you a new lens of compassion for why they sometimes stumble. (More on that in chapter 2.)

But for others, for those who were praised early for their intelligence, their speed, their decisiveness, their ability to get things done, only to find that the very strengths that set them apart later created distance, tension, or misunderstanding, this book

Introduction

may feel like holding up a mirror. It may not be comfortable, but it might be necessary.

So, I say this with humility: it is completely fine if these pages are not for you. That does not make them any less valuable for those who need them. My only hope is that wherever you stand, you find something here that helps you grow or better understand someone you care about.

This is not a book about failure. It is a book about what happens after success; how to transform early promise into a life of sustained growth and meaningful influence. It is about learning the quiet skills too often overlooked: humility, patience, emotional intelligence, and the ability to build allies rather than adversaries.

If you do see yourself in these pages, know this: you are not alone. And your story is not over. Early success need not be a curse. With awareness and practice, it can become the seed of a different kind of success; one that matures, deepens, and leaves behind not just a record of achievement, but a legacy of wisdom.

Long-term success is measured not by early accolades but by planting seeds of integrity and wisdom. I've learned that those same seeds, when tended with awareness, can grow into humility and empathy. What once felt like loss has often become preparation for something deeper. Along the way, I've been shaped not only by my own failures but by the grace of others: mentors who believed in me, family who steadied me, friends and colleagues who reminded me that growth is a team effort, not a solo race.

This book is written for those who reached early heights: the first promoted, the youngest in the room, the overachievers who became benchmarks for others, and then found themselves wondering why the same strengths that once worked now don't.

The purpose/why of this book is to help you reframe that paradox; to turn early success from a ceiling into a foundation for lifelong growth, impact, and meaning.

Over time, I've watched colleagues, teams, and entire organizations make the same pivot—from early advantage to sustainable maturity. The stories in this book reveal what happens when talent learns to evolve. The chapters that follow aren't about failure; they're about the rebirth that follows.

This book is not
a celebration of
early success. It is a
cautionary tale and,
I hope, a guide.

PROLOGUE

A Necessary Confession

This is not easy for me to write. When you read the pages ahead, you may notice stories of rapid advancement, recognition, and early achievement. On the surface, they may sound like boasts, like I am celebrating my own perceived "brilliance" or reliving past glory. But I want to be absolutely clear: this is not my intention.

The truth is that I write these words not from a place of pride, but from a place of humility, and no small amount of regret. I have spent decades wondering why the career that began with such promise did not continue to flourish as I hoped, why the upward trajectory faltered. Why, despite my best intentions, did I find myself misunderstood, resisted, or even undermined by colleagues and peers?

For years, I chalked it up to jealousy or politics. Only later did I realize that much of the struggle stemmed from the very strengths that had once propelled me forward. What I thought would always serve me had, in ways I didn't see, also limited me. What seemed "right" in the moment often proved quietly destructive to relationships and long-term success.

To admit this is embarrassing. To put it on paper is terrifying. But it is necessary. Because I suspect there are others like me: people who were told they were destined for success, praised for being ahead of their peers, who learned to solve problems quickly and outpace those around them, yet later found themselves isolated, stalled, or even pushed out.

This book is not a celebration of early success. It is a cautionary tale and, I hope, a guide. I aim to shine a light on a dynamic that is rarely discussed: how strengths can become weaknesses, how speed can create distance, and how early triumphs can unintentionally plant the seeds of later failure.

I do not write as an expert looking down, but as a fellow struggler reaching across. If you recognize yourself in these pages, know that you are not alone. My story is not meant to glorify but to humanize, not to impress but to confess. Vulnerability is freeing. The very transparency that once embarrassed me has become the bridge that connects me to others walking similar roads.

A Necessary Confession

It is my hope that by exposing my own blind spots and mistakes, I can help others avoid the same pitfalls and, maybe even, redeem some of the lessons before it's too late.

Here is a hard truth: failure teaches more than success ever will.

CHAPTER 1

The Curse of Early Success

The Glory Days That Came Too Soon

When I look back at the earliest years of my career, the story reads like a case study in effortless triumph. I was barely out of college, in my early twenties, entering at the lowest rung of the organizational ladder. Within months, I was producing more quickly, with fewer errors, and with sharper insights than peers who had been there for years.

It wasn't just competence; it was velocity. Where others hesitated, I acted. While they waded through endless drafts, I delivered finished work that exceeded expectations. My education had trained me for this. College had been a relentless grind of projects under impossible deadlines. While classmates pulled three or four all-nighters a week, agonizing over the "perfect" solution, I had already discovered a secret: there is rarely one perfect answer. There are many good ones. My skill was not in agonizing, but in quickly spotting a viable path and executing it with confidence.

Research on choice overload shows that too many good options can cripple decision-making, while swift selection among sufficient alternatives preserves clarity and momentum. Cognitive psychologists emphasize that **heuristics**—simple, "good enough" shortcuts—frequently outperform exhaustive optimization in complex environments. In fact, empirical data from professional chess, a domain of strategic, high-stakes choices, finds that faster decisions often yield better outcomes when compared to bestmove benchmarks.

This discovery and approach gave me two things: freedom and results. I worked less but achieved more. Professors rewarded my clarity and speed, classmates admired my efficiency, and, before long, employers did the same. Promotions followed. Awards came. By my early twenties, I was already supervising large staffs and leading high-profile projects. The narrative was cemented: this was a man destined to succeed. Looking back, I fit the cliché of being labeled "most likely to succeed, but I now see how that label hid dangers I didn't understand. But beneath the accolades, something subtle and dangerous was happening, something I didn't see until decades later. My early success had become my greatest handicap.

The Hidden Trap of Being "Most Likely to Succeed"

At first, success builds confidence. That's natural, and necessary. But too much early success can also build something else: **complacency and unintentional arrogance.** When your first attempts are rewarded, when your instincts are validated again and again, you start to believe two things that will later betray you: That you don't need to keep learning as much as others. And, that your ways of seeing the world—your own natural strengths— are not just one way of many, but the best way. I didn't know it at the time, but I had stepped into a psychological trap well documented by researchers. Decades of studies show that when children or young adults are praised for **ability** rather than **effort**, they grow fragile in the face of setbacks.

Psychologist Carol Dweck famously demonstrated this in her work on mindset: ability-praised students shy away from challenges, while effort-praised students embrace them. Praise of ability creates a fixed identity: "I succeed because I'm gifted." But gifts can wither if not sharpened. My promotions, my awards, my recognition, they were all ability praise at scale. They fed a narrative that I was different, that I was better. And once that belief takes hold, humility becomes harder to practice, and growth becomes easier to neglect.

Success Without Failure Is a Poor Teacher

Here is a hard truth: **failure teaches more than success ever will.** But when you succeed too quickly, you are robbed of the formative failures that ground and guide a career. Early failures, when embraced, teach resilience, humility, and adaptability. They reveal blind spots. They build empathy. They remind you that effort matters as much as talent.

Research bears this out. A study published in Nature (2019) examined scientists who narrowly missed out on early-career grants versus those who narrowly won them. Counterintuitively, the "losers" went on to outperform the winners over the long run. Why? Because the setback forced them to adapt, persist, and refine their work. Early success had lulled the winners into complacency, while early failure forged resilience in the losers. I was one of the "winners." I never learned the resilience lesson…at least, not early enough.

Why Being Right Isn't Enough

The mistake of early success is thinking that results speak for themselves. They don't. People do. In every workplace, human dynamics—jealousy, pride, insecurity, self-preservation—are as real as performance metrics. But because I was focused on outcomes, I underestimated these forces. I thought my better, quicker, more efficient solutions would be welcomed with open arms. Instead, they were received as a threat. What I failed to see is that success is not just about the work you produce; it is about the way you make others feel while you produce it. If your success makes others feel small, they will resist it, even sabotage it.

And here lies the curse: early success trains you to trust your methods, but it blinds you to the invisible costs of those methods on relationships.

The Chapter's Lesson

If you are someone who succeeded early, who was told you were gifted, who climbed fast, who set yourself apart…beware. The very things that lifted you may also be the same things that will later hold you back.

The Curse of Early Success

Early success builds confidence, but confidence without humility calcifies into arrogance. Early achievements build reputation, but reputation without growth stagnates into irrelevance. And natural strengths, if unexamined, become overused weapons that wound the very allies you need.

The first step in overcoming the curse is this: **recognize that being talented and being trusted are not the same thing.**

Leadership isn't about choosing between power and empathy. It's about mastering the dial between them.

CHAPTER 2

The Agentic-Communal Dial: Leading with Strength and Balance

Two Modes of Leadership

Every leader operates between two fundamental modes: **Agentic** and **Communal**. **Agentic** leadership is about drive, direction, and standards—it propels things forward. **Communal** leadership is about empathy, connection, and inclusion—it keeps things together. Each strength mode is a legitimate source of power. Both are necessary. Yet either, when overused or isolated, can become a liability.

Agentic leadership acts when others hesitate. They set a course, make decisions without consensus, and insist on excellence. In moments of uncertainty, this clarity becomes invaluable. People crave direction and confidence. But over time, untempered Agentic energy can overwhelm. The leader's voice grows louder than all others, until eventually, there are no other voices left.

Communal leadership builds loyalty and engagement. It listens deeply, seeks understanding, and creates psychological safety—the space where people can speak freely, admit mistakes, and contribute new ideas. Yet when overextended, Communal energy can drift into avoidance. Empathy turns into hesitation. The desire for harmony eclipses the need for progress. Both modes, unchecked, distort strength into imbalance.

Natural Strengths Can Amplify the Trap

Agentic energy wins quick victories; Communal energy builds lasting ones. The art of leadership lies in knowing when to engage which—and how to blend them wisely. But here's the hard truth: almost no one achieves this balance naturally. Each of us is born with an inclination toward one mode and a deficiency in the other. One flows easily, the other feels unnatural and awkward.

Throughout this book, I reference my own patterns of strength. We all have them: consistent ways of thinking, feeling, and acting that shape both our success and our struggles. In my case, my wiring is unmistakably Agentic.

The Agentic-Communal Dial

My Agentic Strengths

If you, too, are an Agentic high achiever, you may recognize yourself in this list:

- **Strategic:**
  Quickly sees pathways, options, and implications.

- **Self-Starter:**
  Translates ideas into action; prefers progress over waiting.

- **Assertive:**
  Willing to take charge, make decisions, and confront issues directly.

- **Driven:**
  Measures worth through accomplishment and tangible results.

- **Loyal:**
  Values authentic connection within a small, trusted circle.

These Agentic strengths fueled my early success. They produced rapid results and earned recognition.

But over time, they also created distance. My quick wins became someone else's quiet humiliation. My clarity felt like criticism. My drive exhausted people. What seemed like efficiency to me sometimes looked like exclusion to others. Eventually, their silent resentment grew into active resistance.

I spent much of my career operating almost exclusively in the Agentic mode: fast, decisive, precise, accountable. Those qualities accelerated my rise but also set limits I couldn't see. My leadership toolbox was filled with instruments of performance, but light on the tools of patience, empathy, and trust.

My Lesser, Communal Strengths

Where my Agentic strengths dominated, my Communal abilities lagged behind. These weren't weaknesses, just muscles I hadn't developed. If you're wired like me, you might recognize your "weaker" strengths in this list:

- **Flexibility:**
  The ability to adapt and take things as they come.

- **Personal Insight:**
  Understanding and appreciating people's unique qualities.

- **Collaboration:**
  Seeking common ground and minimizing unnecessary conflict.

- **Inclusion:**
  Ensuring others feel seen, valued, and part of the team.

- **Empathy:**
  Sensing the emotions of others and responding with understanding.

The Misunderstanding of "Soft Skills"

When I first learned that these were my "weakest" strengths, I confess I quietly celebrated. They felt foreign—almost irrelevant—to the world I knew. Results were rewarded, not sensitivity.

For years, I viewed these traits as distractions from performance. That belief, I would later realize, was at the heart of my challenge.

- **Empathy?** I often thought, "I don't enjoy managing my own stress. Why would I want to feel someone else's?" It felt inefficient, even indulgent.

- **Flexibility?** I saw it as a drift. I preferred to chart the course, not ride the current.

- **Collaboration?** I equated it with compromise—teams talking in circles while the clock ticked.

- **Inclusion?** Of course, I valued fairness, but not at the expense of the slowed momentum of dragging someone along that just doesn't belong.

- **Personal Insight?** I appreciated people's uniqueness but had little patience for emotional nuance.

And therein lay the problem. These "softer" Communal strengths were not optional; they were essential to transforming early promise into enduring influence. I didn't just undervalue them. I didn't know *how* to practice them.

When colleagues told me to "be more empathetic" or "listen better," I understood the words but not the mechanics. How exactly does one *do* empathy? What does it look like in a meeting, in conflict, or under pressure?

For those with a more balanced blend of Agentic and Communal strengths, and for those naturally wired for connection, these behaviors are obvious, simplistic, and even intuitive. For Agentic leaders like me, they must be learned step by step, habit by habit. They are far from obvious, simplistic, or intuitive.

Translating Communal Strengths into Action

Telling an Agentic performance-driven leader to "slow down," "listen more," or "get along" is like telling a sprinter to "just enjoy the jog." It's conceptually simple but practically complex. Without translation into clear, observable behaviors, the advice is meaningless.

This book aims to make the abstract tangible—to translate the innate strengths of Communal leaders into actionable disciplines for Agentic ones. Because it's not enough to admire soft skills, we must operationalize them.

For years, I treated Communal strengths as secondary, maybe "nice-to-have" qualities, rather than strategic assets. It took repeated disappointment and honest reflection to realize that the most effective leaders weren't just decisive; they were trusted. They didn't just achieve results; they multiplied them through others. That insight changed how I define strength itself.

The New Leadership Equation

As the workplace evolves, leadership success depends less on dominance and more on dexterity, the ability to dial between two complementary forces: strength and connection. Agentic energy without empathy becomes control. Communal energy without direction becomes chaos. Authentic leadership lives in the tension between the two.

The lessons that follow are not confined to my personal wiring. They apply to anyone who's ever felt the pressure of early success or the disorientation of stalled momentum. By understanding your own default setting on the Agentic–Communal dial—and learning how to modulate it—you can lead with both confidence and compassion.

These pages help you not only identify your natural mode but also expand your capacity for its counterpart, turning unbalanced strength into balanced influence.

The Chapter's Lesson

Leadership isn't about choosing between power and empathy. It's about mastering the dial between them.

Never mistake early wins for permanent mastery.

CHAPTER 3

Complacency and the Dangers of Completion

The Subtle Decay of Growth

Early success doesn't just change how others see you; it changes how you see yourself. When your instincts are validated and your work applauded, it's easy to believe that growth is optional. After all, if what you're doing works, why change it?

For me, this shift was subtle.

Early in my career, I was hungry for knowledge. I mastered technical skills, kept up with industry trends, and pushed myself to understand not just the what but the why behind every project. But as I rose into leadership, I made a dangerous assumption: **I no longer needed deep, hands-on knowledge.** My staff could handle that. My job was to oversee.

At first, this logic seemed sound. But over time, it created a widening gap. My industry evolved rapidly, becoming more technical, more specialized, more complex. My hands-on knowledge atrophied while my staff grew. What began as a delegation strategy ended in obsolescence. I had largely stopped learning. And once you stop learning, you start slipping…slowly, silently, but inevitably.

The Psychology of Completion

Why does this happen? Psychologists call it the **complacency effect.** Studies show that when we experience success on a task, the satisfaction of "completion" can actually reduce our motivation to improve or seek feedback.

Success, ironically, teaches us to stop.

One field study on repeated competitions found that winners often underperformed in future rounds compared to losers, because success bred comfort, while loss bred urgency. Success felt like an endpoint; failure felt like fuel.

This explains why people who succeed too early often plateau. They mistake the finish line for the starting line.

Complacency and the Dangers of Completion

Strengths and the Complacency Trap

Agentic strengths, like mine, are especially vulnerable to this:

- **Strategic + Self-Starter** = Together, these create confidence in quick solutions. Once validated, the temptation is to believe every problem can be solved just as quickly, reducing patience for deeper learning.

- **Driven** = The drive to "move on to the next goal" makes pausing to learn or reflect feel inefficient.

- **Assertive** = Decisiveness, once rewarded, risks becoming rigidity. You stop entertaining alternative views because you've been right before.

Individually, Agentic strengths are powerful. Together, unchecked, they create the illusion that growth is unnecessary.

The Cost of Stopping Too Soon

When I reflect on my career, I see this clearly. My early trajectory was fueled by my ability to learn and absorb everything faster than my peers. My later trajectory faltered because I abandoned that hunger. I thought my role was to manage, not master.

The cost was steep: My relevance in fast-moving industries declined. My authority rested on past successes, not current expertise. My peers began to surpass me, not because they were more talented, but because they kept learning while I stopped.

This is the quiet tragedy of complacency: you rarely notice it until others do. Even then, it is all too easy to dismiss.

The Chapter's Lesson

Early success plants the seeds of complacency. The applause convinces you that you've arrived, when in fact you've only begun. The cure is vigilance: **never mistake early wins for permanent mastery.** Keep learning even when you don't have to. Stay hands-on, even when delegation is possible. Measure growth by new skills, not just new titles. Because in the long arc of a career, those who adapt will outlast those who arrived early but stopped moving.

Here's the paradox: people don't always need to be right, they always need to feel heard.

CHAPTER 4

The Social Backlash of Success

Success Is Never Just About You

We like to imagine success as a solitary achievement. We picture the lone innovator, the brilliant leader, the prodigy whose talent speaks for itself. But in real workplaces, success is never just about you, it is always about how others experience you.

This was one of the hardest lessons I am still learning. My Agentic quick thinking, decisiveness, and relentless drive were personal strengths. They made me efficient. They made me effective. They also made me, unintentionally, threatening. Where I saw contribution, others saw competition. Where I saw improvement, others saw insult. Where I saw efficiency, others saw arrogance. Over time, this perception gap led to growing challenges...many of them unseen.

The Psychology of Jealousy and Self-Preservation

Social psychologists describe two forces at work here:

- **Social Comparison Theory (Festinger, 1954):** People constantly measure themselves against others. When they feel outperformed, they feel threatened. Instead of admiration, they often respond with envy or resentment.

- **Self-Preservation Instincts:** In organizational settings, people protect their status, turf, and credibility. A colleague who consistently "outshines" them can feel like a danger to their role, reputation, or future opportunities.

This is why outperforming others doesn't always win you friends. In fact, the higher you rise and the faster you succeed, the more you trigger these psychological defense mechanisms in those around you. **It isn't rational. It isn't fair. But it is real.**

The Social Backlash of Success

My Agentic Strengths as Triggers

Looking back, I now see how my Agentic strengths—so celebrated early on—were double-edged swords:

- **Strategic:** I saw solutions quickly. To me, that was helpful. To others, it felt as if I were dismissing their ideas before they finished speaking.
- **Self-Starter:** I pushed for immediate action. To me, that was progress. To others, it felt like I was steamrolling.
- **Assertive:** I spoke directly. To me, that was clarity. To others, it felt intimidating.
- **Driven:** I set relentless standards. To me, that was excellence. To others, it felt as if I were making them look bad.
- **Loyal:** I sought honesty and depth. To me, that was connection. To others, it felt like exclusivity.

None of these interpretations was my intent. But perception matters more than intention.

The Curse of Early Success

The Pattern of Undermining

Over time, I noticed a troubling pattern. In nearly half of the jobs I held later in my career, I was eventually forced out, not because of poor results. While the outcomes were often strong, my relationships told a different story just as frequently—and that ultimately mattered more.

I was, in hindsight, being undermined. Peers who felt diminished by me worked quietly to erode my standing. They whispered doubts. They resisted my initiatives. They aligned with others against me. I had always chalked this up to jealousy; people resenting my capabilities. There was truth in that. But the deeper truth was this: **I had played a part in provoking it.** My success had made others feel insecure. My style had made them feel unappreciated. And when people feel insecure and unappreciated, they don't become allies. They become adversaries.

The Human Need to Feel Heard

Here's the paradox: people don't always need to be right, but they always need to feel heard. When colleagues feel ignored, dismissed, or overshadowed, their loyalty erodes. It doesn't matter if your solution is better, faster, or smarter. If it makes them feel small, they will resist it.

This is where many high achievers with Agentic strengths tend to stumble. We assume that producing results is enough. But results alone don't secure allies. Relationships do. And relationships require the Communal strengths of patience, empathy, and recognition; qualities that don't come naturally to many quick thinkers and self-starters.

The Chapter's Lesson

The social backlash of success is real. It isn't enough to deliver excellence; you must do so in a way that preserves the dignity of those around you. Otherwise, your success will be met with resistance, not support.

The first step is awareness: recognize that your speed, decisiveness, and confidence can trigger insecurity in others. **The second step is adjustment:** learn to slow down, to listen, to credit, to soften. Because in the long run, success is not a solo sport. It is a coalition. And coalitions are built not just on what you achieve, but on how you make others feel while achieving it.

Being perceived
as collaborative
is just as important
as actually
being effective.

CHAPTER 5

Slowing Down without Losing Speed

Why Perception Matters More Than Pace

If there's one lesson I wish I had learned earlier, it's this: being perceived as collaborative is just as important as actually being effective.

In my career, I prided myself on speed. I thought quickly, decided quickly, and acted quickly. And often, I was right. But what I didn't realize was that speed, without consideration for how it appeared to others, often looked like arrogance.

Here's the paradox: you don't actually have to slow your thinking down; you just must **slow your presentation down**.

To others, it's not your speed of thought that matters; it's whether they feel included, respected, and heard.

The Curse of Early Success

"He's Not a Learner"

In a previous role, I attended a large-group teleconference that included a senior executive I had not yet met.

Afterward, he made a comment to my supervisor that stunned me: "He's not a learner, is he?" When my supervisor relayed this to me, I was both insulted and confused. I had never interacted with this leader before. How could he possibly reach such a sweeping and damaging conclusion in a single teleconference?

Looking back, I realize the impression I left must have been one of unintentional arrogance. My natural Agentic strengths of decisiveness, confidence, and conviction had likely come across as being a "know-it-all" rather than as someone curious and open to growth. Without even realizing it, I had projected certainty when humility would have served me better.

That single comment—"not a learner"—felt like a dagger. But over time I've come to see it as a mirror. Even if unfair in its bluntness, it reflected what others might perceive when one leads with too much conviction and not enough openness. Unintentional relational costs can be high and unseen; how others can interpret our behavior in ways we never intended.

The Illusion of Patience

If you think quickly, you don't have to change that. But you do need to create the appearance of patience.

Practical Techniques

- **The Two-Second Rule:** After someone finishes speaking, silently count "one, two" before you respond. This tiny pause signals that you are considering their words, even if you already knew where they were going.

- **Echo Before Add:** Repeat a portion of what they said before sharing your view: "So you're saying the timeline could slip if we add that step. That's a good point. What if we also…" This shows that you valued their input, even if you pivot immediately.

- **Ask Before Tell:** Before offering your solution, ask: "How do you see this playing out?" or "What obstacles do you anticipate?" Even if you already know the answer, this creates space for them to own part of the solution.

- **Slow the Body, Not the Mind:** Your nonverbals speak louder than your words. Nod. Lean in. Keep an open posture. Resist cutting people off. These micro-signals of attention calm others, even if your mind is racing ahead.

How Some Agentic Strengths Need Restraint

Certain Agentic strengths are especially vulnerable to "fast perception":

- **Strategic:** You spot patterns instantly. But blurting them out makes others feel obsolete. Practice letting the team surface options, even if you already know the answer.

- **Self-Starter:** You thrive on action. But moving too quickly makes others feel bulldozed. Use your energy to summarize the consensus before pushing forward.

- **Assertive:** You speak with clarity. But too much directness can feel like intimidation. Replace "Here's what we should do" with "Here's one option, what do you think?".

Slowing Down without Losing Speed

- **Driven:** You raise the bar relentlessly. But if you don't pause to acknowledge progress, others burn out. Celebrate before you escalate.

- **Loyal:** You value deep, honest dialogue. But in group settings, this can look like favoritism. Make sure everyone feels equally included.

The goal is not to suppress your Agentic strengths, but to **channel them more deliberately** so they inspire trust instead of tension.

Making Others Feel Heard

Here's the truth: people don't just want solutions, they want recognition. When you make people feel heard, three things happen: **They lower their defenses.** They stop seeing you as a rival. **They buy into solutions.** Even if your idea prevails, they'll own it with you if they feel included. **They become allies.** Instead of undermining, they begin to support.

Simple Phrases That Work

- "That's a good insight. I hadn't thought of it that way."
- "Help me understand your perspective a little more."
- "You're closer to this process than I am. What's your take?"
- "That's helpful. Let's build on it."

These phrases aren't filler, they are bridges. They turn sharp edges into open doors.

Changing without Threatening

One of the hardest lessons for driven self-starters is this: **improvement can feel like criticism.** When you suggest a new way of doing something, you may think you're helping. But others may hear: "You've been doing it wrong."

To avoid this pitfall: **Frame changes as experiments.**

Instead of "Here's the better way", say: "Let's test this approach alongside what we're doing and compare results." **Credit others when possible.** "Building on Sarah's point, what if we tried…" **Use "we" language.** "How can we streamline this?"

instead of "Here's how you should do it." This subtle reframing transforms your improvements from threats into collaborations.

Exercises for the Reader

- **The Listening Audit:** For one week, track how many times you cut someone off or finish their sentence. The goal isn't zero, but to raise awareness.

- **Reframe Drill:** Take a recent directive you gave (e.g., "We need to do this faster"). Rewrite it as a collaborative question ("What would it take for us to make this faster?")—practice reframing.

- **Praise Bank:** Each day, intentionally credit at least one colleague in front of others. Note how it shifts the atmosphere.

- **Patience Practice:** In your next meeting, identify one moment to deliberately hold back your answer until three others have spoken. Compare the dynamic.

The Chapter's Lesson

You don't need to slow your thinking; you need to slow your delivery. When you give people time, echo their input, frame changes collaboratively, and credit their contributions, you transform perception. Instead of being seen as arrogant, you are seen as inclusive. Instead of being resented, you are respected. Instead of being undermined, you are supported.

And that shift, perception over pace, can make the difference between early success that fizzles and long-term success that endures.

Stop seeing others
As obstacles and start
seeing them as allies
waiting to be activated.

CHAPTER 6

Turning Rivals into Allies

The Silent Undercurrent

Early success doesn't just make you stand out, it makes others feel left behind. And in any workplace, people don't always celebrate being outpaced. They protect themselves. They defend their reputations. They protect their turf.

This is the social backlash of success at its most personal: **jealousy.** Sometimes it's visible in eye rolls, clipped comments, or subtle resistance. Other times, it operates in silence, in back channels, in alliances formed without you, in opportunities quietly withheld.

I didn't recognize these signals early in my career. I assumed peers would welcome Agentic strengths of better solutions, faster execution, and higher standards. Instead, my success often triggered their insecurity. Where I saw improvement, they saw exposure. Where I saw contribution, they saw competition. The result? Undermining. Quiet sabotage. And eventually, career setbacks that blindsided me. But jealousy doesn't have to be fatal. With awareness and skill, you can turn it into something else: respect. Even partnership.

Recognizing the Early Signs of Self-Preservation

If you want to turn rivals into allies, the first step is noticing when rivalry begins. Look for these cues:

- **Withdrawal:**
  Once-talkative colleagues stop volunteering ideas in meetings.

- **Defensiveness:**
  They justify past approaches instead of exploring new ones.

- **Back-channeling:**
  You hear about alternative conversations or decisions happening without you.

- **Passive resistance:**
  Deadlines slip, initiatives stall, and support quietly evaporates.

- **Tone shifts:**
  Jokes become sarcastic; praise becomes faint.

These are not random quirks of personality. They are signals that you've triggered social comparison or threatened someone's self-preservation instinct.

The Triggers

For Agentic high achievers, the triggers are often predictable:

- **Strategic:**
  Spotting the answer too quickly makes others feel behind.

- **Self-Starter:**
  Pushing for immediate action makes others feel dismissed.

- **Assertive:**
  Speaking bluntly makes others feel exposed.

- **Driven:**
  Setting higher standards makes others feel inadequate.

- **Loyal:**
  Building deep bonds with some colleagues can leave others feeling excluded.

When people feel "less than" around you, they stop seeing you as a teammate and start seeing you as a rival.

Strategies to Disarm Jealousy

The key to disarming rivalry isn't in denying your Agentic strengths; it's in finding a balance with Communal strengths and reframing your ideas. Hence, they feel like a shared advantage instead of a personal threat.

Give Away Credit Generously: If your idea works, don't hoard the spotlight. Attribute it to shared effort:

- "This builds on what Mark suggested last week."
- "Our team really sharpened this idea together."

This costs you nothing but earns allies.

Ask for Expertise You Already Know: Yes, you may already have the answer. But asking for someone else's take validates their importance.

- "You're closer to this than I am. What's your view?"
- "I trust your eye for detail. What do you think?"

This flips the dynamic: instead of overshadowing them, you elevate them.

Frame Improvements as Collective Progress:
It turns your suggestion from a critique into an invitation.

- Don't say: "Here's a better way."

- Do say: "How can we make this even stronger together?"

The difference is subtle but profound.

- **Convert Threat into Partnership:** If someone seems threatened by you, pull them closer, not further away. Give them ownership of part of the project. Let them lead a sub-initiative. Make them feel indispensable to the win.

- **Acknowledge Feelings, Not Just Facts:** Sometimes, the best way to diffuse rivalry is to name what's happening without judgment:

    o   "I get the sense this change feels like it undercuts your work. That's not my intent. How do we make sure it strengthens your role?"

This transforms tension into trust.

From Competitors to Collaborators

One of the most powerful reframes you can make is this: **stop seeing others as obstacles and start seeing them as allies waiting to be activated.**

The resistant coworker who drags their feet? They might just need recognition. The peer who constantly defends their turf?

They might become your fiercest partner if you affirm their expertise. The one who undercuts you in meetings? They may just need to be brought into the spotlight with you.

When you treat potential rivals as allies-in-waiting, you change the relational battlefield. You stop fighting against people and start fighting alongside them.

Exercises for the Reader

- **Rival Radar:** List three colleagues with whom you feel tension. For each, write one strength or expertise they bring that you can affirm in your next interaction.

- **Credit Shift:** In your next meeting, make it a goal to publicly credit at least two people, even for small contributions.

- **Inclusion Pivot:** Identify one initiative where you tend to "run ahead." Pause and ask a peer to co-lead part of it. Watch how it changes the dynamic.

- **Language Swap Drill:** Take three recent sentences you've said (e.g., "We need to do this faster"). Rewrite them in inclusive language ("What would it take for us to speed this up together?").

The Chapter's Lesson

You can't stop people from feeling jealousy. But you can prevent jealousy from hardening into rivalry.

When you share credit, invite input, frame progress as collective, and elevate others, even when you don't need to, you transform potential enemies into allies. And allies, not adversaries, are the foundation of lasting success.

Early success
Rewards soloists.
Long-term success
rewards conductors.

CHAPTER 7

The Invisible Skills of Sustained Success

The Limits of Speed and Talent

In the first act of your career, speed and talent carry you. You think quickly, decide quickly, and act soon. You outpace your peers, and results follow. But in the second act of your career, those same Agentic strengths—when operating alone—begin to lose their power. Why? Because success over decades isn't about how fast you think or how much you know. It's about how well you relate, how deeply you listen, and how effectively you build coalitions of trust.

These Communal strengths are less visible. They don't win awards. They don't get measured on performance reviews. But they are the difference between someone who flames out after early promise and someone who sustains influence into their later years.

The Successor

Later in my career, I worked under a newly promoted CEO. She was freshly elevated from within the company, and stepping into a new role. Because of my deep respect for her predecessor, I naturally transferred that same loyalty to her. At first, our relationship was strong. She was refreshingly open about her learning curve and candid about her mistakes, qualities I admired. For several years, we worked well together.

But eventually, something shifted. Distance crept in between us, and I couldn't understand why. She often counseled me to "slow down." I frankly had no idea what she meant. To me, that sounded absurd. Slowing down meant producing less revenue, fewer wins, and fewer results. Why would any CEO want that?

Only later did I realize her caution wasn't about outcomes, it was about pace. I believe that my relentless drive was exhausting her. She needed more time to reflect and process, and my pace was unintentionally overwhelming. On top of that, other colleagues—threatened by my influence—fueled her insecurities and whispered doubts about my motives. I will never forget the day she looked me in the eye during a meeting and asked: "Eric, are you trying to get my job?"

Her question stunned me. Though I had never considered such a thing, I later realized how my unchecked drive and pace could easily have created the impression that I was a rival rather than an ally. What began as trust and respect had turned into suspicion and distance. I still believe she was an outstanding leader, and I wish I had been more self-aware and might have preserved that relationship.

Communal Strengths: The Slow Virtues

I like to call Communal strengths the **slow virtues** because they counterbalance the natural impulses of early achievers:

- **Humility:** The willingness to admit you don't know, to keep learning, and to let others shine.

- **Patience:** The discipline to let conversations, processes, and people unfold at their own pace.

- **Emotional Intelligence:** The ability to sense how others feel, and to adjust your approach accordingly.

- **Coalition-Building:** The skill of turning groups of individuals into allies who want you to succeed.

Without these, purely Agentic strengths and drive can easily backfire. With them, those same strengths become unstoppable.

Humility: The Anchor of Growth

Humility is not thinking less of yourself; it's thinking of yourself less. For high achievers, humility feels unnatural. If you've been rewarded for being the one with the answer, it's hard to admit you don't have it. If you've been praised for moving fast, it feels wrong to wait. But humility is what reopens the door to growth when early success tempts you to stop learning.

Practices to Build Humility

Say "I don't know" more often. Paradoxically, it earns more respect than pretending. **Ask for help.** Not because you can't do it, but because it honors the expertise of others. **Mentor downward.** Teaching others reminds you of your own unfinished journey.

Patience: The Art of Letting Things Breathe

Patience doesn't mean inaction. It means creating space for others to catch up, contribute, and buy in. Your **Self-Starter** strength pushes you to move now. But teams don't move at the speed of your mind. They move at the speed of trust. And trust requires time.

Practices to Build Patience

- **The Two-Second Rule:**
  Wait before responding.

- **The Third Voice Rule:**
  Hold your input until at least two others have spoken.

- **Build pauses into projects:**
  Don't sprint every initiative; insert reflection checkpoints where teams can regroup.

Emotional Intelligence: Reading the Room

Emotional intelligence is the Communal invisible radar that tells you when someone feels unheard, threatened, or undervalued. Without it, you're blind to the forces that can undermine you. For example, your **Assertive** strength makes you decisive, but without emotional intelligence it can come across as domineering; and your **Strategic** talent makes you see solutions quickly, but without emotional intelligence it can look like dismissiveness.

Practices to Build Emotional Intelligence:

- **Check body language:**
  Crossed arms, silence, or flat expressions often signal resistance.
- **Name emotions:**
  "I sense this change feels uncomfortable. Can we talk through what's behind that?"
- **Solicit private feedback:**
  People reveal more one-on-one than in groups.

Coalition-Building: From Soloist to Conductor

Early success rewards soloists. Long-term success rewards conductors. Coalition-building means creating groups of people who want you to succeed because your success benefits them too. This requires giving away credit, elevating others, and ensuring everyone feels like a stakeholder. Your **Loyal** strength helps here. You crave deep, authentic relationships. Use that to your advantage by forging alliances not just with close confidants but with those who feel most distant from you.

Practices to Build Coalitions

- **The Credit Multiplier:**
  Publicly tie your wins to others' contributions.

- **The Inclusion Habit:**
  Invite someone outside your usual circle into a project.

- **The Shared Battle Frame:**
  Always frame challenges as "us vs. the problem," not "me correcting you."

Exercises for the Reader

- **Humility Journal:** Each week, write down one thing you admitted you didn't know and one thing you learned from someone else.

- **Patience Practice:** In your next meeting, deliberately hold back your input until three people have spoken. Note how it changes the tone.

- **EQ Radar:** At the end of the day, jot down two moments when you sensed tension in others. Ask yourself: what triggered it, and how could I have responded differently?

- **Coalition Map:** Draw a map of your team or organization. Circle your allies. Put a square around those who may feel threatened by you. Pick one square to move toward allyship this month.

The Chapter's Lesson

Speed will get you noticed. Talent will win you accolades. But neither will sustain you for decades. What sustains you are the slow virtues: humility, patience, emotional intelligence, and coalition-building. These are invisible skills. They don't show up on résumés. They don't win trophies. But they are the foundation of lasting influence. When you master these, your early success stops being a curse and becomes a seed; one that can grow, not just in the short arc of your first act, but across the long arc of a life well-lived.

The curse of early success can be broken, but not by trying harder at what made you successful in the first place.

CHAPTER 8

Tools for Transformation

From Awareness to Action

By now, you've seen the hidden traps of early success: complacency, arrogance, relational backlash. You've also seen the "slow virtues" that can counteract them: humility, patience, emotional intelligence, and coalition-building.

But understanding isn't enough. Transformation only happens when insight becomes practice. This chapter is designed to give you **concrete tools**—scripts, reflection prompts, and exercises—that will help you reframe your strengths, handle jealousy, and create alliances instead of enemies. Think of this chapter as your **field guide**.

Navigating Jealousy and Self-Preservation

One of the most painful lessons of my career came from a peer who held a powerful position in the company. At first, I believed that if I worked hard, contributed innovative ideas, and delivered results, my efforts would be valued naturally. Instead, I encountered a dynamic I had never anticipated: deliberate undermining.

This peer would routinely dismiss my suggestions in meetings, often labeling them as too progressive, incompatible with the company culture, or simply bad ideas. What stung most was that a year or two later, he would reintroduce the very same ideas, repackaged as his own, and promote them as fresh strategies.

When I privately pointed out that I had proposed these improvements earlier, I thought I was defending my contributions. In reality, I was threatening his authority. My insistence on being recognized only fueled his resentment and drove him to work tirelessly behind the scenes, eroding my reputation with half-truths and innuendos.

Eventually, his efforts succeeded. Despite my strong performance and undeniable results, I was forced out. In hindsight, I see now that I could have handled this very differently. Rather than insisting on credit, I might have chosen to let him present the ideas as his own, recognizing that the bigger "win" was seeing the improvements implemented, not whether my name was attached to them. By letting him take ownership, I might have preserved the relationship and turned a rival into an ally.

The lesson here is difficult but essential: in environments where power and ego are at stake, the wisest path is sometimes to surrender personal credit in service of the greater outcome. Protecting relationships, even if it means swallowing pride, can secure far more influence and long-term success than fighting for recognition ever will.

Reframing Your Strengths

Your strengths are not the problem; they are your greatest assets. The challenge is learning how to express them in ways that **invite collaboration** rather than trigger defensiveness. Here's how to reframe common strengths that often backfire:

- **Strategic**
    - Old style: "Here's the answer."
    - New style: "Here are a few paths I see. What do you think?"
- **Self-Starter**
    - Old style: "Let's do it now."
    - New style: "What's the first small step we could take today?"

- **Assertive**
    - Old style: "This is the direction we need to take."
    - New style: "Here's one direction I see. What are the risks you'd watch for?"
- **Driven**
    - Old style: "We need to raise the bar."
    - New style: "We've accomplished a lot. How do we build on it?"
- **Loyal**
    - Old style: Building bonds with a few close colleagues, leaving others feeling excluded.
    - New style: Making a point to include new voices, then deepening trust over time.

Reflection Prompt: Which of your strengths tends to create tension with others? How could you reframe its expression using more inclusive language?

Tools for Transformation

Scripts for Defusing Rivalry

Jealousy and self-preservation are inevitable when you stand out. These scripts can help you defuse them in real time:

- **When someone feels overshadowed:** "You've been driving this work from the start. My suggestion is just to build on your foundation."

- **When resistance shows up:** "I can tell this idea doesn't sit right. What concerns do you see that I might be missing?"

- **When you sense turf protection:** "I know this is your area of expertise. I'd love your guidance on how best to approach it.

- **When credit is due:** "This breakthrough wouldn't have happened without your insight."

Daily Habits to Build Slow Virtues

Transformation doesn't come from occasional insights. It comes from daily habits. Here are practical routines for each slow virtue:

- **Humility Habit:** Once a day, ask someone, "What's your perspective?", and listen without interrupting.

- **Patience Habit:** In meetings, wait for at least two others to speak before sharing your view.

- **Emotional Intelligence Habit:** After a tough interaction, jot down what emotion you think the other person was feeling. Train your radar.

- **Coalition Habit:** Once a week, publicly credit someone else's contribution, preferably in front of their boss or peers.

The Rival-to-Ally Framework

When you notice someone moving into rivalry mode, use this four-step framework:

- **Spot the Signs:**
  Withdrawal, defensiveness, resistance, sarcasm.

- **Name the Value:**
  "You bring expertise in X that I really respect."

- **Invite Ownership:**
  "Could you lead this part of the project?"

Tools for Transformation

- **Share Credit:**
  "This success is because of the way [name] pushed us forward."

Journaling Prompts for Reflection

Use these prompts weekly to anchor your growth:

- Where this week did I unintentionally rush ahead of others?

- When did I make someone feel heard? What impact did it have?

- Who seemed threatened by me? How did I respond?

- Where did I celebrate progress instead of moving immediately to the next challenge?

- Which slow virtue (humility, patience, emotional intelligence, coalition-building) did I practice most this week? Which did I neglect?

A Personal Challenge: The 30-Day Reset

For the next month, commit to one practice per week:

- **Week 1:**
  Practice the Two-Second Rule in every conversation.

- **Week 2:**
  Give away credit at least once per day.

- **Week 3:**
  Ask for input from someone you usually overlook.

- **Week 4:**
  Pause before raising the bar; celebrate first.

At the end of 30 days, review your journal. You will notice subtle but powerful shifts: less resistance, more support, stronger relationships.

The Chapter's Lesson

The curse of early success can be broken, but not by trying harder at what made you successful in the first place. It is broken by transforming your approach: reframing your strengths, defusing rivalry, practicing the slow virtues daily, and creating allies rather than enemies.

Tools for Transformation

These tools are not theoretical. They are practical, repeatable actions anyone can practice, starting today. And if you commit to them, you'll find that early success doesn't have to be a curse at all. It can become the foundation of a second act, one marked not just by achievement, but by influence, respect, and legacy.

Success teaches you.
what works.
Failure teaches you
what doesn't,
and in that gap
lies innovation.

CHAPTER 9

Embracing Setbacks As Fuel

The Failure I Didn't Have Soon Enough

If I could rewrite my career, I wouldn't erase my failures. I would move them earlier. Early in life and work, success came easily. I rose quickly, earned awards, led big projects, and rarely faced defeat. Each victory reinforced my sense of capability. Each accolade told me I was "different." But beneath the surface, something essential was missing: the refining power of failure.

When failures did come later in my career: being forced out of various roles, being undermined by peers, watching opportunities slip away, I wasn't ready. I hadn't built the muscles to metabolize failure into resilience. Instead of being a natural part of my growth, those failures felt catastrophic. What I've since learned is this: **failure is not the opposite of success. It is the engine of sustained success.**

Why Failure Matters More Than Success

Psychological research confirms what experience eventually teaches: early setbacks often build stronger long-term outcomes.

As we saw earlier with the Nature grant study, early failure often fuels long-term excellence. Compared to those who narrowly won, the "losers" went on to publish more impactful work over the next decade. Why? Because failure forced them to adapt, persist, and refine. The winners, cushioned by early success, often stagnated.

This pattern plays out far beyond academia. In business, sports, and creative fields, those who experience manageable failures early build the resilience, humility, and adaptability that fuel later greatness. Success teaches you what works. Failure teaches you what doesn't, and in that gap lies innovation.

Why Early Successors Struggle with Failure

For those of us who succeeded early, failure feels uniquely destabilizing. Why?

- **Fragile Identity:** When your worth is tied to being "gifted," failure feels like identity collapse, not just a temporary setback.

- **Lack of Practice:** Without small failures along the way, your resilience muscles are underdeveloped.

- **High Visibility:** Early success puts you on a pedestal. When you fall, more people are watching, and the humiliation feels sharper.

- **Pride:** Confidence hardens into arrogance, making it difficult to admit mistakes or ask for help.

The irony is that those who struggle early often become stronger later, while those who soar early often falter when turbulence arrives.

Reframing Failure As Fuel

The path forward isn't to avoid failure, it's to **reframe it as fuel.** For early achievers, this requires a fundamental mindset shift:

From **threat** → to **teacher**

From **end point** → to the **starting point**

From **personal flaw** → to **growth opportunity**

Instead of asking, "What does this failure say about me?" ask, "What is this failure giving me that success never could?"

Strengths and the Failure Reframe

Each of your top strengths has a shadow side when it comes to failure, but also a growth opportunity:

- **Strategic:** You may assume you'll always see the best path. Failure teaches humility, that not every pattern is visible at first.
- **Self-Starter:** You move fast. Failure teaches discernment, that not every action is worth immediate execution.
- **Assertive:** You speak with authority. Failure teaches empathy, that sometimes people need reassurance more than direction.
- **Driven:** You measure worth by productivity. Failure teaches rest, that your value isn't only in output.
- **Loyal:** You seek deep trust. Failure teaches breadth, that allies beyond your inner circle can be essential.

Embracing Setbacks As Fuel

Practical Tools for Turning Setbacks into Strengths

- **The Debrief Ritual:** After every setback, ask:
    - What did I control?
    - What was outside my control?
    - What can I do differently next time?
- **Failure Resume:** Write a résumé not of your achievements, but of your failures. For each, note what it taught you. This normalizes failure as part of your story.
- **Controlled Risk Practice:** Each month, deliberately take on a project or challenge where failure is possible. Stretch yourself into discomfort.
- **The 24-Hour Rule:** Allow yourself 24 hours to feel the sting of failure. After that, force yourself into reflection mode. Don't wallow. Learn.

Stories of Fuel from Failure

Think of the innovators, leaders, and creators you admire. Almost all have failure at the root of their success stories:

The Curse of Early Success

- Thomas Edison tested over 1,000 prototypes before inventing the light bulb.
- Oprah Winfrey was fired from her first TV job for being "unfit for television."
- Steve Jobs was ousted from Apple before returning to lead its greatest renaissance.

What distinguished them wasn't early brilliance. It was their capacity to metabolize failure into fuel.

Exercises for the Reader

- **Reflection:** What is one failure in your past that still feels like shame? How could you reinterpret it as training for resilience?
- **Action:** Identify one area of your work where you've been playing it safe. This month, choose a bolder option, even at the risk of failure.
- **Ally:** Share a recent failure openly with a colleague or friend. Watch how it builds trust rather than diminishes respect.

Embracing Setbacks As Fuel

The Chapter's Lesson

Failure is not your enemy. It is your teacher. If early success shielded you from failure, you may feel unprepared when setbacks arrive. But failure, reframed, can give you what success never did: humility, resilience, empathy, and adaptability.

Your task is not to avoid failure, but to **fail forward**; to let each misstep refine you into someone more capable, more grounded, and more trusted. Because in the long run, it is not the one who succeeds first who endures. It is the one who learns best from failure.

Authority without relevance erodes quickly.

CHAPTER 10

Rediscovering Hands-On Learning

When I Let Go Too Soon

In my early career, I knew my craft inside and out. I was fast, effective, and deeply involved in the details. That hands-on mastery was the engine of my early success. But as I rose into leadership, something shifted. I believed my role was no longer to do the work but to manage it. I delegated technical tasks to my staff and assumed that a broad, generalist view was enough. At first, it worked. Projects ran smoothly. My team carried the load.

But slowly, almost invisibly, the gap widened. The industry advanced. New tools emerged. Processes became more technical. My staff grew sharper, while I grew more distant. What I thought was smart delegation became dangerous detachment. Eventually, I recognized that my credibility rested too heavily on past reputation rather than on fresh, relevant knowledge. And that's a fragile place for any leader.

The Leadership Trap: Managing vs. Mastering

Many early achievers fall into this same trap. Once promoted, they assume leadership is about oversight rather than engagement. They stop building skills, assuming their value lies only in vision and delegation. But here's the truth: **authority without relevance erodes quickly.** When leaders disconnect from the work: They lose credibility with their teams. They miss signals of industry shifts. They rely too heavily on others for expertise. They stagnate while the field evolves around them. Delegation is necessary. Detachment is fatal.

Why Hands-On Matters for Long-Term Success

Even as a leader, staying close to the work keeps you:

- **Credible:**
  Teams trust leaders who understand their challenges firsthand.

- **Relevant:**
  Industries evolve; leaders who keep learning remain future-proof.

- **Resilient:**
  Hands-on knowledge gives you options when structures shift.

- **Engaged:**
  Curiosity fuels energy, and energy fuels leadership.

The goal isn't to micromanage. It's to stay sharp enough that your vision is grounded in reality.

The Agentic Strengths Connection

The Agentic strengths that led to early success make this trap especially likely, but they also hold the key to reversing it:

- **Strategic:** You naturally look at the big picture. But without periodic, in-depth dives into the details, your strategies lose accuracy.

- **Self-Starter:** You prefer starting things rather than maintaining them. But committing to learning new tools keeps you agile.

- **Assertive:** You speak with confidence. But confidence without updated knowledge risks sounding out of touch.

- **Driven:** You crave output. But producing only through others can weaken your own learning edge.

- **Loyal:** You build close bonds. Use this to learn directly from team members. Let them teach you.

The shift isn't about doing everything yourself. It's about balancing leadership with curiosity.

How to Rediscover Hands-On Learning

- **Shadow Your Team:** Spend a day sitting alongside someone closer to the ground. Ask them to walk you through their process. Don't correct. Just learn.

- **Take a Tool Test-Drive:** Pick one new platform, tool, or process in your industry. Learn it at a beginner level. Not because you'll use it daily, but because it keeps your instincts sharp.

- **Stay in the Arena:** Choose one part of your work where you remain hands-on. Whether it's drafting a pitch, analyzing data, or writing a strategy doc, keep your skills alive.

- **Ask "Teach Me" Questions:** Invite your team to explain trends, challenges, or new methods. This does two things: it keeps you learning, and it makes them feel valued as experts.

- **Learn Outside Your Comfort Zone:** Growth often comes from the periphery. Attend a conference, read outside your discipline, or take an online course. Stay curious.

Stories of Leaders Who Stayed Hands-On

- **Satya Nadella (Microsoft CEO):** Known for his technical curiosity even as CEO, often asking engineers to walk him through code-level decisions.

- **Angela Merkel (German Chancellor, trained physicist):** Carried her scientific rigor into politics, often drilling into technical detail to earn credibility.

- **Elon Musk:** Whatever one thinks of his style, his insistence on understanding technical details earns respect from engineers, even when controversial.

These leaders balance vision with detail, proving that hands-on learning isn't about micromanagement, it's about credibility.

Exercises for the Reader

- **Reflection:** When was the last time you learned a new tool, process, or skill in your field? What's the risk if you don't?

- **Action:** This week, schedule one "shadow session" with a colleague or team member. Let them teach you something.

- **Growth:** Choose one area where you've grown detached. Commit to re-engaging hands-on for the next 30 days.

The Chapter's Lesson

Early success often tempts us to step away from the work too soon. We delegate, then detach. But sustained success requires staying close enough to remain credible, relevant, and adaptable.

Leadership is not just vision; it is grounded knowledge. The best leaders are not above the work; they are beside it. They never stop learning, even when they no longer "have to." Rediscovering hands-on learning is not regression. It is resilience. It ensures that early success is not your peak, but the foundation for a career of lasting influence.

Even when you are right, if others feel ignored or diminished, they will resist you.

CHAPTER 11

Practicing Patience and Inclusivity in Collaboration

Why Collaboration Requires a Different Speed

I used to believe collaboration meant combining the best ideas and choosing the strongest path forward. What I didn't understand was that collaboration isn't only about ideas, it's about experience.

When you think quickly and move decisively, collaboration can feel inefficient. You already see the solution while others are still defining the problem. So, you jump in, offer your conclusion, and move forward. The result? You save time, but you often lose people.

Collaboration doesn't just ask what you decide, it asks how you decide. And in the long run, people will judge your leadership less by the brilliance of your answers and more by how valued they felt in the process.

The Legacy Project

Another pivotal lesson came not from a superior, but from a peer who had staked much of their career identity on what they proudly called their "legacy project." This was an initiative they had championed for years, nurturing it from idea to implementation.

By the time I was asked to take over, it was clear the project wasn't just another assignment. It was deeply personal for them, something they wanted to be included in and remembered for.

I came in with the same energy and strengths that had carried me through so many other challenges: drive, creativity, and a relentless push to improve. I worked hard to refine processes, suggest efficiencies, and raise the bar on what the project could become. From my perspective, I was helping. From theirs, I was threatening the very thing they wanted to preserve. What I failed to grasp at the time was that this project was no longer primarily about innovation. It was about recognition and closure. It was their name, their career, and their story written into the DNA of the work.

My efforts, however well-intentioned, made them feel overshadowed and diminished, as if their "legacy" were being rewritten by me rather than honored through them. The friction grew quietly but steadily. Where I saw opportunities, they saw interference. Where I offered improvements, they heard criticism. Eventually, the relationship soured, and with it, the potential for collaboration.

In hindsight, I realize that if I had slowed down, listened more carefully, and asked what mattered most to them, I could have found a way to support their goals without unintentionally stealing the spotlight.

The lesson was sobering. Not every situation calls for transformation. Sometimes the best contribution is restraint; allowing others to shine, even when you see ways to make things better. By honoring their need for legacy, I could have gained an ally. Instead, I lost one, all because I misread what success meant to them.

The Cost of Impatience

Here's the irony: even when you are right, if others feel ignored or diminished, they will resist you. Sometimes consciously, sometimes unconsciously. They'll delay, disengage, or even undermine your efforts. Impatience isn't just a personal quirk. It comes with organizational costs: projects stall because people feel disinvested. Trust erodes when colleagues sense they don't matter. Your reputation shifts from "brilliant problem-solver" to "difficult to work with." What you gain in speed, you lose in influence.

Why This Hits Early Successors Hard

For those who succeed early, impatience is reinforced by results. You move faster, produce more, and earn promotions. You learn to believe speed = success. But as responsibilities grow, the equation changes. The higher you rise, the more success depends on collective buy-in, not individual brilliance. Speed alone stops working.

The Strengths Connection

Several of Agentic strengths create this tension:

- **Strategic:** You see patterns immediately. Others feel "left behind" in your conversations.

- **Self-Starter:** You want to move now. Others feel bulldozed.

- **Assertive:** You speak directly. Others feel intimidated.

- **Driven:** You push for output. Others feel exhausted.
- **Loyal:** You seek deep bonds. Others outside that circle feel excluded.

Your strengths are not flaws; they are accelerators. But accelerators without brakes cause collisions.

How to Practice Patience in Collaboration

- **Create the Illusion of Slowness:** You don't have to slow your mind, just your delivery.
    o Pause before responding.
    o Echo what someone said before adding your view.
    o Ask clarifying questions, even if you already know the answer.

This signals respect, even if you've already solved the puzzle.

- **Prioritize Psychological Safety:** People contribute when they feel safe. To build that safety:
    o Thank people for their input, even if you disagree.

- o   Avoid interrupting. Let them finish.
- o   Frame disagreements as curiosity: "Help me see how you got there."

When people feel safe, they stop protecting themselves and start engaging fully.

- **Reframe Speed as Inclusion:** True speed is not about reaching decisions faster. It's about reaching decisions that stick. A decision made quickly but resisted later is slower than one made inclusively and executed with full commitment. Ask yourself: Am I moving quickly, or am I moving effectively?

- **Use Language that Invites, Not Closes:**

  - o   Replace: "Here's what we should do." With: "One option I see is this, what are your thoughts?"
  - o   Replace: "We need to move faster." With: "What would it take for us to speed this up together?"

Small shifts in phrasing make others feel like partners, not obstacles.

- **Celebrate Before Escalating:** Achievers often skip celebration. But recognizing progress builds energy.
  - Pause to name what's working before pushing for what's next.
  - Publicly highlight contributions before setting new goals.

This transforms pressure into motivation.

Practical Exercises

- **The Third Voice Rule:** Hold your input until at least two others have spoken. Notice how it changes the room.

- **Mirror and Add:** Before offering your idea, restate someone else's perspective first.

- **Inclusion Audit:** After a meeting, ask yourself: Who spoke most? Who didn't? What can I do next time to invite quieter voices?

- **Pace Check:** In your next project, deliberately insert one "reflection checkpoint" before execution. Let the group catch up.

The Chapter's Lesson

For early achievers, impatience is both a strength and a weakness. It propels you forward but alienates others. The secret isn't to stop thinking quickly; it's to create the space for others to join you.

Collaboration is not measured by how fast you decide, but by how many people feel ownership in the decision. And ownership is built not on brilliance, but on patience, inclusivity, and respect. When you practice these invisible disciplines, your strengths stop alienating and start multiplying. You stop moving alone and start moving together.

High achievers face a unique trap: their early wins reinforced the belief that outcomes matter more than feelings.

CHAPTER 12

Developing Emotional Intelligence and Self-Awareness

Why EQ Matters More Than IQ

Early success often creates an overreliance on intellect, strategy, and speed. You've been rewarded for being right, fast, and decisive. But as roles expand and responsibilities deepen, those qualities aren't enough. What separates effective leaders from frustrated ones is not intelligence, it's **emotional intelligence (EQ)**.

Emotional intelligence is the ability to:

- **Recognize your own emotions and triggers** (self-awareness).

- **Regulate your responses** (self-management).

- **Perceive what others are feeling** (social awareness).

- **Adapt your behavior to build trust and alignment** (relationship management).

Without EQ, Agentic strengths like Strategic, Drive, or Assertiveness become blunt instruments. With EQ, they become precision tools.

A Leader I Greatly Respect

Earlier in my career, I had the privilege of working under a CEO and founder whom I respect more than perhaps any leader I've ever known. He was wise, kind, and genuinely human in his leadership. During my tenure, I contributed to a period of historic growth for his company, and my results were undeniable.

One day, however, he pulled me aside and said something I'll never forget: "Eric, I get the sense that you think results are more important than people's feelings." I laughed out loud, assuming he was joking. But he wasn't. He was entirely serious.

Trying to recover, I explained that feelings mattered when everyone was aligned, but if someone dug in their heels and resisted leadership's chosen direction, then their feelings were irrelevant compared to achieving results. He listened, unconvinced.

At the time, I dismissed his comment as the "softening heart of an aging man." Surely, objective results mattered more than ever-changing subjective feelings, especially when their feelings led to behavior that occasionally blocked results.

Now, with the benefit of hindsight, I realize how wrong I was. My Agentic strengths and drive had blinded me to the importance of the Communal strength of bringing others along. Results without relational investment come at too high a cost. In the long run, my inability to see this truth contributed to my eventual ouster from that company. One of my lasting regrets is knowing that a leader I still admire deeply may think less of me because of my shortsightedness.

Why Early Agentic Successors Struggle with EQ

High achievers face a unique trap: their early wins reinforced the belief that outcomes matter more than feelings. After all, grades, promotions, and recognition usually come from performance, not patience. But when people sense you don't "get them," they won't follow, even if you're objectively correct. In fact, the more successful you are, the more others subconsciously look for cracks in your humility, hoping to level the playing field. This is why emotional intelligence is not optional for long-term success. It's your antidote to envy, pride, and self-preservation instincts in others.

Self-Awareness: The First Step

Self-awareness is the discipline of noticing what's happening inside you, before it spills outside. Questions to ask yourself daily: What emotions am I carrying into this meeting? Where am I feeling impatient, threatened, or overlooked? What reaction am I most likely to trigger in others? How might my strengths unintentionally overwhelm this situation? Self-awareness is like checking your dashboard before driving. It doesn't slow you down, it prevents crashes.

Reading the Room

Social awareness requires noticing not just words, but signals.

- **Body language:** Who is leaning back, crossing arms, or withdrawing?
- **Tone shifts:** Did someone's energy drop when you spoke?

- **Participation:** Who stopped contributing after you weighed in?

These cues aren't noise, they're feedback. They tell you when pride, insecurity, or self-preservation instincts are at play.

Regulating Yourself in Real Time

It's not enough to notice, you must adjust.

Practical strategies include:

- **Pause before responding:** Give space for others' voices.
- **Name the tension:** "I sense some hesitation. What are we missing?"
- **Slow your delivery:** Speak with deliberate pacing, even if your thoughts are racing.
- **Redirect the spotlight:** "That's an interesting point, let's explore it further."

These micro-adjustments prevent defensive walls from going up.

Turning Awareness into Influence

Emotional intelligence is not about softening your brilliance. It's about amplifying your impact by keeping others engaged. When people feel understood, they:

- Stop competing with yourself.
- Lower their defenses.
- Offer their best ideas openly.
- Transform from rivals into allies.

The goal is not to avoid conflict; it's to manage emotions so that conflict becomes productive rather than destructive.

Practical Exercises

- **The Emotional Debrief:** At the end of each day, ask:
    - When did I feel impatient, annoyed, or defensive?
    - How did I manage it?
    - How did others react to me?

Write short reflections to build awareness patterns.

- **360 Listening Drill:** In your next meeting, spend the first 10 minutes saying not a word. Instead, observe—note who defers, who dominates, and who hesitates. You'll be surprised by what you see when you're not trying to win the conversation.

- **Trigger Mapping:** List 3 recurring situations that frustrate you (e.g., indecision, over-detailing, pessimism). For each, plan a regulated response (e.g., curiosity rather than rushing, encouragement rather than critique). This builds muscle memory for patience.

- **Ask for Feedback:** Choose a trusted peer or mentor and say:

    o "What's one thing I do that makes people feel heard?"

    o "What's one thing I do that shuts people down?"

Feedback is a mirror, sometimes uncomfortable, but essential for self-awareness.

The Chapter's Lesson

Emotional intelligence is not a luxury skill, it is the defining quality of lasting leadership. Without it, strengths create friction and success breeds resentment. With it, strengths create trust and success breeds loyalty.

Self-awareness and social awareness give you the ability to notice insecurity, jealousy, pride, and self-preservation as they emerge. Regulation and relationship management let you turn those instincts into collaboration rather than rivalry.

Don't just win,
win with others.

CHAPTER 13

Building Allies, Not Enemies

The Ultimate Test of Leadership

Success is not measured by how many ideas you had, how quickly you solved problems, or even how many promotions you earned. It's measured by how many people you lifted with you, and how many doors remain open after you leave. In other words, the final stage of maturing beyond the curse of early success is this: **do others see you as a competitor or as an ally?**

Why Rivals Arise in the First Place

Throughout this book, we've named the forces that turn colleagues into rivals:

- **Jealousy:** Resentment of your speed, clarity, or recognition.
- **Pride:** The need to protect their own reputation.

- **Fear:** Worry that your success diminishes their security or standing.
- **Self-preservation:** A defensive instinct to avoid being overshadowed.

These reactions are rarely about you personally or your strengths, they're about what you represent. To someone else, you symbolize change, risk, or the possibility of being left behind.

Recognizing this truth frees you from taking resistance personally.

The Three Shifts to Build Allies

- **Shift from proving to empowering:** Stop trying to prove you're right or the smartest in the room. Instead, use your insight to help others look good. A simple pivot: "Here's one way to see it, but I think your angle connects it better to our goals."
- **Shift from speed to pacing:** Move at the pace of trust, not just the pace of results. Sometimes slowing down builds more lasting momentum than rushing ahead alone.
- **Shift from spotlight to reflection:** The leader who shines the light on others multiplies

influence. Celebrate peers publicly. Credit them often. When they feel seen, envy has no soil to grow in.

Practical Tactics for Turning Rivals into Allies

- **Name Shared Wins Early:** Frame projects around collective outcomes: "If we succeed, we all benefit." This reduces zero-sum thinking.

- **Offer Protection:** Tell colleagues privately, "I've got your back." People ally with those who lower their risk.

- **Build Micro-Trust:** Small gestures—inviting input, asking advice, giving credit—build compound interest in relationships.

- **Neutralize Threat Perceptions:** When others fear being overshadowed, make it clear their expertise is indispensable: "Your perspective is what makes this work credible."

- **Transform Opposition into Ownership:** If someone resists, assign them responsibility for part of the solution. Critics become co-authors when they hold the pen.

The Curse of Early Success

Recognizing When It's Not About You

One of the most liberating insights you'll ever gain is this: **not every rival can be converted.** Some people will remain threatened no matter what. In those cases, your task is not to win them. It's meant to minimize their ability to erode trust while continuing to elevate those around you.

But most people, especially those who begin as wary competitors, can be disarmed and eventually turned into loyal allies if you lead with humility, patience, and recognition.

Leaving a Legacy of Allies

When people look back at your leadership, they won't remember how fast you were or how many times you were right.

They'll remember: Did you make me feel safe? Did you help me grow? Did you give me credit? Did I become more because I worked with you? That's the measure of enduring leadership. That's how brilliance stops being a curse and becomes a gift.

Practical Exercises

- **The "Rival List" Audit:** Write down three people who may view you as competition. For each, ask:
    - What might they fear losing?
    - What value do they bring that I can affirm?
    - How can I reposition them as a partner this month?

- **Public Credit, Private Support:** Make a habit of praising someone publicly once a week and offering protective support privately once a week. Both deposits grow relational equity.

- **Alliance Mapping:** Visualize your network as allies, neutrals, and potential rivals. Your goal: shift one person per quarter from "neutral or rival" into "ally." Over years, this builds a deep bench of loyal supporters.

Final Reflection: From Curse to Gift

The "curse" of early success is that it can isolate you; make you the target of envy, pride, and rivalry. But when you harness your strengths with self-awareness and emotional intelligence, you transform that curse into a gift.

You become the leader whom others don't just admire for being successful but appreciate for making them successful. And that is the legacy that outlives any single achievement.

The Chapter's Lesson

The capstone of overcoming the curse of early success is this: **don't just win, win with others.** Use your brilliance to elevate, not overshadow. Use your speed to include, not exclude. Use your achievements to protect, not threaten. Allies multiply your influence. Enemies shrink it. And the difference is almost always in your hands.

If early success taught me the power of strength.
Later struggle taught me the necessity of connection.

CHAPTER 14

Balance

The Cost of Overuse

Looking back, I see that my early success came from mastering the Agentic mode, while my later challenges came from failing to balance it with the Communal one. What I once dismissed as "soft" was actually *stabilizing*.

My pace, decisiveness, and standards were essential, but they needed to be anchored in empathy, not resistance to it. Most organizations don't fail because their leaders are weak; they fail because their leaders overuse the very strength that once made them successful.

Learning to Turn the Dial

With experience comes discernment, the ability to sense when a situation calls for strength, and when it calls for understanding.

Leadership Dial Control

SITUATION	TURN UP	HOLD STEADY	KEY BEHAVIOR
Crisis or turnaround	Agentic	Communal	Be decisive and visible; explain *why* before moving on.
Innovation or collaboration	Communal	Agentic	Listen widely, then narrow decisively.
High performance environment	Balance	—	Maintain standards and autonomy equally.
Low trust or fatigue	Communal first	Agentic next	Rebuild credibility through empathy, then drive execution.

The point isn't to choose one mode over the other: it's to learn how to shift smoothly between them.

High Standards + High Support

The most effective leaders I've met hold people to exacting standards *and* give them the support to meet them. High standards without high support create fear. High support without high standards creates complacency. Authentic leadership lives at the intersection, where clarity and compassion coexist.

The Humility Hinge

The single quality that allows a leader to adjust without losing authenticity is humility. Humility says, *I don't have to be right to stay strong.* It invites learning, tempers ego, and keeps the dial free to move. Humility doesn't make a leader softer; it makes them steadier.

The Integration Point

I used to believe I needed to trade one style for another: to replace my drive with empathy, my focus with inclusion. I now see that was the wrong frame.

The goal isn't to become less intense; it's to become *stronger through balance.* The best leaders are fully human; decisive when clarity is needed, compassionate when connection is broken, humble enough to know which is which.

A Final Reflection

If early success taught me the power of strength, later struggle taught me the necessity of connection. Authentic leadership isn't the pendulum swing between the two. It's learning to hold them both at once. Strength without empathy can build walls. Empathy without strength can build confusion. But strength *with* empathy builds trust, and trust, in the end, is what makes leadership last.

Let your legacy be this: You left no enemies behind, only allies, and a trail of others made stronger by your presence.

EPILOGUE

From Shadow to Light

When you began this journey, you may have carried a weight you couldn't quite name. A sense that your early success, once a blessing, had somehow become a source of friction, misunderstanding, or even isolation. You may have wondered: Why do my strengths sometimes make things harder instead of easier? Why do others resist when I only want to help? Why does being good at what I do feel like a burden? This book has given that feeling a name: **the curse of early success.** But here's the truth: it was never a curse. It was a gift waiting to be understood.

The Journey You've Taken

In **the early chapters**, you learned why brilliance, speed, and achievement can sometimes draw jealousy, pride, and self-preservation instincts from others. In the **middle chapters**, you saw how self-awareness and emotional intelligence transform those shadows into wisdom. In the **practical**

chapters, you discovered how to slow down, listen deeply, and make others feel valued, even when your instincts want to rush ahead. And in the **final capstone**, you learned the greatest lesson: that leadership is not about being the smartest or the fastest, but about creating allies, multiplying others' strengths, and leaving a legacy of trust.

The Light Beyond the Shadow

The curse of early success was never about you being too much. It was about others not knowing how to respond. And now, with awareness, you can meet their fear with reassurance, their pride with humility, their self-preservation with generosity. You can step into rooms not as the fastest voice, but as the calmest presence. You can transform rivals into allies. You can leave places better than you found them, not only in outcomes, but in relationships.

So here is my invitation: The next time you feel misunderstood, pause. The next time you sense jealousy, listen. The next time you feel the urge to prove yourself, reflect instead: How can I make this person feel safer, stronger, and more valued? Do this, and the curse dissolves. The shadow recedes. And your early success, once a lonely burden, becomes a lifelong gift. Not just for you. But for everyone you touch.

Closing Thought: Your brilliance was never the problem. How you use it determines whether it isolates or multiplies. Let your legacy be this: you left no enemies behind, only allies, and a trail of others made stronger by your presence.

www.ingramcontent.com/pod-product-compliance
Lightning Source LLC
Chambersburg PA
CBHW031424210526
45464CB00005B/2043